"The ministry o
and authority. This t
rising up to proclaim

Dr. Carroll Thompson, Ph.D.
Author, CFNI Instructor, 40 years

"Like the first book, Rev. Anthony Dee is very complete and presents the information very well. The program itself has the markings of being born out of the heart of Jesus. To me this is the missing link in the church of the in the U.S. today. It will serve to bring the saints to a more mature level of faith as this is certainly our mandate in Scripture. *The Adopt-A-Family Follow-Up* system is a clear-cut way of doing what we are called to do normally as believers, but seem to have forgotten about."

Sr. Pastor Ken Leleux, Ph.D.
Glorious Church Worship Center
ICFM Regional Director

"'What do you do for follow up?' is the question that evangelists frequently hear. In this power-packed book, Rev. Anthony Dee helps to answer this important question. Jesus told us to catch and teach, not catch and release. This book will teach you how to turn converts into disciples by implementing the *Adopt-A-Family* strategy."

Daniel King
Crusade Missionary-Evangelist
King Ministries, Tulsa, Oklahoma.

"After the revival with Rev. Anthony Dee, including Sunday morning services, New Beginnings International Church has definitely moved to a new level of faith. We are believing God for healings and miracles more than ever, and we have no intentions of going back."

Sr. Pastor Don Couch
New Beginnings International Church, Ft. Worth, TX.

"This book is a much needed practical resource that I pray will find its way into the hands of believers, outreach directors, and pastors who desire to reach those who don't know Christ in their own community."

Scott Hinkle
S.H.O.M., CFNI Presbyter and Instructor, Dallas, TX.

"It is with great delight that I highly endorse this new resource from Rev. Anthony Dee! I believe that you will glean both practical wisdom and a godly perspective as Rev. Anthony Dee shares from his personal experience, as well as his passion for the lost. It is not often that you find a resource that offers both pragmatism and heartfelt experience, but this is a resource that offers both! Rev. Anthony Dee does a wonderful job of equipping the saints in establishing discipling relationships."

Michael Cole
CFNI Director of Relational Development

"Our church used the *American Missions: Soulwinner's Manuel* by Rev. Anthony Dee and the concepts were so plain and simple that our people embraced them and used them with joy. We even had to order more of them for a later group to study and use."

Pastor Gary Woodard
Mount Pleasant Christian Center, Assemblies of God
San Jose, California

A NOTE FROM THE EDITOR

Rev. Anthony Dee knows what it is to minister under the anointing of God. His heart to give Jesus all the glory is just one of the reasons why he stays in high demand as a guest speaker in Bible Schools and local churches around the world. The healing testimonies from his teaching and ministering sessions are numerous and consistent. He knows how to flow with the Holy Spirit, and as a result, God's power is there to accomplish what only God Himself can do.

I have known Rev. Anthony Dee for several years. We first became acquainted when I helped him reedit and update his first book, *The American Mission: Soulwinner's Manual*. Even as I began the work on his book, I was quite surprised and impressed by this young man's wisdom and anointing.

As I began to look at his new book, *Adopt-A-Family Follow-Up*, I could see the same kind of wisdom—a practical, but biblical approach in successfully teaching us how we can reach our neighbors and communities for Christ. The great news for some, who don't consider themselves to be "Evangelists," is you don't actually have to preach. All you are required to do is make the initial contact, find out what they might need, and then work with the church in meeting that need. The service, and more importantly, the brotherly love that is shown to these individuals becomes a godly example of the true, deep love God has for them.

Rev. Anthony Dee has a sincere heart for God. He is motivated by God's love to demonstrate how easy it is for a Christian to show that same kind of love to anyone … whether they are a stranger or a relative.

You will be blessed in reading this book. You will be even more blessed if you take what he teaches and put it into practice. You will be following the command Christ Himself gave to us. "Go ye therefore …"

Polly Harder
Director of Publishing
Christ For The Nations/Creative Press

ADOPT-A-FAMILY
FOLLOW-UP

*Bridging the Gap Between
Outreach and Discipleship*

by
REV. ANTHONY DEE

Published by:
CREATIVE PRESS
P.O. Box 769000
Dallas, Texas 75376-9000

Copyright © 2013 Rev. Anthony Dee
ISBN#978-0-89985-396-3

THANK YOU

A special thank you to all those who contributed in making this book a reality.

Leanne and "The Splawn Family"
Gene and Diane B.
Joy S.
Benjamin P.
Karen T.
Ed S.
Mom and Dad

Though there is not enough room to name all those who deserve appreciation for their support and prayers in the production of this book, a sincere thank you to you all, as well for your contribution. You know who you are, and Heaven knows who you are.

Thank you all, again.

CONTENTS

Chapter 1

TO ADOPT-A-FAMILY

Terry rushed to answer the phone with her 1-year-old daughter, Ellen, propped up on the side of her hip. After she picked the phone up and sputtered, "Hello, hello?" she immediately felt the tug on her leg. Looking down, she saw that it is from none other than her 3-year-old son, who was desperately clinging to her leg. She turned her attention back to the phone, but all she heard was the dial tone. Sighing, she said to herself, "How can I juggle so many responsibilities with these kids?" Then she heard in a soft whisper, "But will you thank Me for the job your husband has?" She felt her heart twinge. "But why can't he be here when I need him the most?"

Anita awakes to the sound of a child screaming. "Mommy, Mommy, help!" In a daze she stumbles into the kitchen, and says, "What is it; what is it?" Looking down, she sees that her daughter, Maria, has a bloody knee and silverware is scattered all around the floor. The cabinet above the kitchen counter was open, and it was totally evident that someone had been rummaging through it. Maria said, "Mommy, when is Daddy coming home? My knee hurts!" Anita thought to herself, "Why can't she forget about him? Doesn't she realize he's been gone for over a year?" Her eyes began to water. Then little Maria held up a small plastic baggy with some white powder in it. "What's in this bag, Mommy ... sugar?" Anita heard a subtle whisper, "I have a better Way for you."

The realities of life can touch us all. These two mothers are dealing with similar family troubles that are not uncommon to the human experience. What is the answer for these issues? It's different for them both, and yet, the answer is still the same. While the first mother, Terry, only seems to focus on her momentary discomfort, she fails to recognize the blessing of a faithful husband, steady income, and a good church. Although she may feel quite disadvantaged in the moment, her dilemma is by no means as unfortunate as Anita's.

An even sadder reality is that Terry is a born-again Christian, caught up in the rat-race of the everyday life, and the reality that there are hurting and broken families, like Anita's family, seldom crosses her mind. She can't even remember the last time she shared Jesus with someone. Although, if you ask her, she will say she shared Jesus around the time when she got saved at youth camp, which was many years ago.

Whether you can relate to Terry or not, perhaps you can identify with the reality of an epidemic of families who lack a relationship with God in America and around the world. As God has blessed me with the privilege of traveling around the world as a missionary-evangelist, I have experienced one common attitude among believers. This is, a dissatisfaction that families who don't know the Lord are not being reached through conventional church methods.

Could it be that God is awakening the conscience of believers around the world with a universal burden? A statistician in America reports that from year-to-year, Americans are increasingly dissatisfied with "church as usual." Is God stirring this burden up in the peoples' hearts? And if so, what else is He trying to say?

Another common sentiment I hear in my travels around the globe is a desire to get back to what the Bible teaches the Church should look like. When I became born-again and accepted Jesus, after being an atheist many years back, it didn't take me long to realize that there were things I read in the Book of Acts that I did not see anyone in my church doing. "Outreach" programs or events were some of the things I didn't see, and the "discipleship" program was just a class for people who already attended the church regularly. Could God be awakening the hearts of believers in every country to go back to the Book of Acts model as the standard role of Christianity?

Well, where do we go from here? It seems that we are in a dilemma. It's like a highway, where all signs lead to what Jesus said. In Matthew 28:19, it says, "Therefore go and make disciples of all nations, baptizing them in the name of the Father and of the Son and of the Holy Spirit" (NIV). Regardless of the fact that these words were some of the last words He spoke before ascending to Heaven in human bodily form, how many churches and Christian families do you see obeying this Word in your part of the world? Surely, our hearts should be deeply grieved by this reality.

As an American believer, who has faithfully submitted to a senior pastor's leadership since I got saved, I have seen many things that didn't seem right in the Church. Though I knew the best response was always to pray and not to get offended, the reality of the extreme quantity of discipleship books and materials that are available in proportion to the actual effective discipleship programs that were visibly seen in the local church seemed alarmingly low.

In America, we have no shortage of discipleship curriculums that believers can utilize once they have established a relationship with someone in the community. If just having more curriculums available for the new disciple to study was the answer to our discipleship famine in America, then the problem should have already been fixed by now. However, unfortunately, anyone who is willing to be honest about it would admit that discipleship and spiritual maturity in America has been steadily declining.

If a discipleship curriculum is not the answer, then what is? One thing I observed, as I was entrusted with the task of teaching and equipping the students in the Evangelism Student Ministry at Christ For The Nations Institute, was the reality that many believers want to do something; they just don't know where to get started. Then, I realized the majority of our material on discipleship programs in America focuses on a curriculum that you can use to 'walk-through' with a new believer, once they already have an established relationship.

However, as for how to establish a discipleship relationship with someone in the community in the first place, the materials seem to be exceptionally lean. The problem isn't the lack of teaching material to use in how to 'walk-through' with a new believer. The problem is the lack of teaching that actually teaches a believer how to get the discipleship relationship established in the first place. We can't put the cart before the horse.

Unless believers are equipped to know how to build a relational bridge with those families who are in the community, they will never have a chance to walk through any kind of curriculum with them, regardless of how good it is; period.

This brings me to the purpose of the Adopt-A-Family Follow-Up Format. It is to teach families how to bridge the gap between the outreach and the discipleship program through a family relationship.

I wholeheartedly believe that God inspired me to write this material as an answer to the widespread problem of believers and families who don't know practical ways of how they can get started in a discipleship program. My prayer is that as you read this book, you will read it with an open heart, being sensitive to the Holy Spirit, to speak to you about how this approach of serving those in the community can open up doors to share Jesus with lost families through an extended, loving relationship with them.

Chapter 2

A POWERFUL REVELATION

So maybe you're wondering how I got interested in discipleship. Well, you would have to know something about my history. As I already mentioned in chapter one, I am a former atheist. Though it may sound strange, I would regularly attend Bible studies at that time when I was in high school. Though most of my hang-out time was with the super-brainy, evolutionistic, anti-religious, "thinkers," for some reason, they were too depressing to hang around with all of the time. So, consequently, I would also hang around with Christians sometimes for a pick-me-up. They were quite a bit perkier, exciting, and seemed much happier. Looking back in retrospect, I guess I needed that. A common question that I usually get asked is what attracted me to go to Bible studies as an atheist. My answer would be the life-giving atmosphere.

Anyway, so when I got saved, it was a unique experience. I'll never forget one week, when a guy named Mark came into the Bible Study. For some reason, he was way different from any other Christian I had ever met before. In fact, he seemed intense, intelligent, and had a strong conviction about what he believed—even the way he spoke and the way he walked reflected this. This was a completely foreign experience for me. Most Christians, I felt like at that time, were quite unstable. They needed Christianity to prop them up like a crutch, and they also didn't have much of an intelligent answer for anything you asked them about. Now, I am not trying to be negative, but that's actually how I felt as a former atheist. Of course, after getting born-again, I currently believe something completely different.

However, being both intrigued and astonished with Mark, it was only natural for me to gravitate toward him. I desperately wanted to try and figure out why he seemed so incredibly different. I am quite an analyzer, so this conundrum just reeled me in like a fish. One day, as I was just hanging around him, I heard him say he was going to see the movie *Passion Of The Christ*. He said that he was willing to take anyone who wanted to go—they could carpool with him to go and check it out. Since I was just generally interested in hanging around Mark because I was trying to figure out what made him tick, I said, "Sure, I want to go."

A POWERFUL ENCOUNTER

So here I am, a few days later, in the movie theatre watching the *Passion Of The Christ* with Mark. As I watched the movie with Jesus being whipped, beaten, and scourged, the reality of Jesus just hit me. Completely disarmed, I am crying my eyes out, and don't know why. As I watched the reality of Jesus being tortured and carrying the cross, God encountered me in that movie theatre. He supernaturally showed me that Jesus is the Son of God, that He came in human bodily form, and that He suffered and died for my sins. This revelation hit me like a transformational train wreck that I could not resist. I left that movie theatre completely undone. I couldn't wait for someone to invite me to church.

So maybe now you are questioning how that fits in with discipleship? Well, this is how it all works together. Mark was like the unofficial deacon of deacons at his church. I began to attend the services with him on a regular basis after that encounter. From that point on, *Mark and I were always together*.

We did everything at the church together—from sound-engineering, weeding the flowerbeds, plumbing, cementing around the flagpole, and painting. You name it, Mark and I fixed it together. This is how I came to know Jesus, not because of a little church program, but because of someone who took the time to demonstrate to me what it meant to be a follower of Jesus—on a one-on-one basis.

You see, discipleship is something that I know as a Christian because it's how I was birthed into Christianity. Maybe you are like me and have your own "Mark story," too. Well, that's the way it's supposed to be. That's how Jesus set it up. We are all supposed to have that person in our lives who was that "Mark" to me to help us learn what it means to be a Christian. This kind of experience should not be the exception; it should be the rule—that is, biblically speaking.

Furthermore, how would you like to be the "Mark" for someone else who needs Jesus?

After I received Jesus as my Lord and Savior and was discipled by Mark for about two years, I always highly valued spiritual discipleship as a part of God's plan.

Since I became born again over a decade ago, by the grace of God, I have had the privilege of teaching evangelism, outreach, and follow-up courses around the world. I won't go into too much detail about that, but what I will say is this. In all of my experiences sharing the Gospel around the world, I have observed an extreme lack of training on how to transition evangelism into regular, everyday, discipleship relationships. You might have found it to be different where you are. Praise God!

However, I believe that if we were to be honest with ourselves, we would have to admit that most Christians do not even know where to get started when it comes to discipleship. Furthermore, it seems that most of our common approaches to evangelism in our current Church culture rarely teach us how to bridge the gap between the two.

This is the purpose of the Adopt-A-Family Follow-Up format. We want to provide enough information to the believer so we can bridge the gap between evangelism and discipleship.

A POWERFUL REVELATION

An earnest desire to see this change drove me to a

place of prayer. One day, as I was seeking God, He gave me a powerful revelation. It was, "If every family in a local church just discipled one family in the community, the size of any church could double every six months."

I then realized how important this really is. I ask you, "What church-growth program has ever claimed those kinds of results?" I was wondering how the Church could have overlooked such a powerful tool that Jesus Himself gave us. The reason why the local church would double is because every church family who discipled a family of roughly the same size in the community, would not only bring them into the fold, but then the new members, as well as the original members, would be repeating it again. If the program lasted for six months, then the potential would be there to increase the size of the church twice a year, doubling and possibly quadrupling their size.

QUALITY RELATIONSHIPS

I also got the revelation that it takes time for quality relationships to form. A family in the community would require multiple visits over an extended period of time to develop trust and a relationship with a church family. Since there is no way to put that into a formula, we do not know if it would take a week, six weeks, or six months, but if a church family is faithful to serve a family in the community, at least, within a six month timeframe, hopefully, the new family will have joined the church.

The exciting reality of this approach is that no one is

excluded! Many times, when you talk about discipleship or evangelism, Christians typically have a knee-jerk reaction. Instantly, they put up a wall against it in their minds and start rehearsing reasons why it is not their job. It is not necessary to think this way, since everyone has someone they can best relate to within the community.

EVERYONE IS CALLED TO DISCIPLE

In each believing family, there is stage-of-life match with other families in the community. For instance, most families in the community have children, parents, and grandparents. So, this means that Christian grandmothers should not feel excluded from outreaches and discipleship because there will come a time when there will be a grandmother in the community family who will need someone to effectively share with her about the love of Jesus. Furthermore, kids and teenagers from a church family will have the best success sharing Jesus with those of a similar age group.

Jesus never made distinctions in His Word about who should and shouldn't disciple, but He say's to us all in his model of church-growth, "Therefore go and make disciples of all nations, baptizing them in the name of the Father and of the Son and of the Holy Spirit, and teaching them to obey everything I have commanded you" (Matthew 28:19-20 NIV).

Imagine the impact it would have on this generation of children and teenagers for them to see their parents take them on consistent community outreaches to share Jesus with hurting families. What kind of a mark would that leave on the children to see Mom and Dad ministering to hurting families? How would that inspire the kids to be more devoted to the gospel and to God because of the model that their parents have positively demonstrated? A popular saying for child-rearing is, "Kids don't obey what you say ... but they obey what they see you do." How interested are we really in the spiritual maturity of our children, and how are we leading by example in this area? Think of how we deny our young people a life-changing blessing by choosing to leave them at home to play videos games on a day where there is an outreach.

I remember, one time when I was doing a Dynamic Evangelism Equipping series at a church in Harare, Zimbabwe. Part of our outreach was to do a community letter drop to invite families in the area to come to church. This outreach was also geared for those who were faint-of-heart, when it came to outreaches, due to its non-confrontational nature. There were a handful of little kids and some toddlers, who decided to participate in this fun activity. One of the kids, named Kudzi, who was about 6-years-old, would drop a church invitation in each mailbox, and then, he would close his eyes, lift up his hand, and pray over the home. Soon, the other kids followed his example. Those who joined them on the outreach were quite moved in their hearts because of this simple child-like faith they witnessed as they moved from house-to-house.

WE NEED A HEART TRANSPLANT

Unfortunately, for many Christians, they have read the Scripture to "Go and make disciples ..." (Matthew 28:19 ESV) for many years, maybe even 20 or 30 years, and have never made the decision to disciple anyone, yet. Is the problem an intellectual problem or a heart problem? In this book, I will talk about the story of Kevin. He was the first man I ever led to the Lord. I was much younger than he was at the time, and I was only a baby Christian. While only being saved less than two years, God used me to disciple him, and to get him plugged into the local church—all for His glory, of course. If I could do it by the empowerment of the Holy Spirit, while I was just a baby Christian, why can't you?

It's not a matter of one person being better suited for it; it's a matter of one person being willing to cooperate with the Holy Spirit to do it through them. The biggest issue is not competence, but the willingness to trust and rely on the Holy Spirit. Again, there is no way to put this into a formula. This book is not about a formula. It is about many different starting points that help people get going in the right direction. However, ultimately, only the Holy Spirit can do the work of winning souls and true discipleship. Our success in doing so, in the local setting, and in our individual lives, is purely based upon our willingness to cooperate with Him, the Holy Spirit.

One time, while I was in a conversation with Reinhard Bonnke, I asked him, "What are three of the most important things to know about evangelism." One of His responses to me was that "the Holy Spirit is the Master Evangelist." I'll never forget the mark this statement made on my heart.

It has nothing to do with our own abilities, qualifications, or personal glory because the Holy Spirit will work with any willing vessel. Those who are most cooperative with the Holy Spirit will actually see the most fruit and experience the most results. Consequently, Scripture teaches us, "Abide in me, and I in you. As the branch cannot bear fruit by itself, unless it abides in the vine, neither can you, unless you abide in me" (John 15:4 ESV). Those who are not bearing fruit are failing to do so because of a failure to abide in the Holy Spirit. We should pray for believers in the Church today to have two revelations:

1. That believers will have a desire to draw near to the Holy Spirit in prayer, so that He alone can equip and move through them to bring in a mighty harvest of families.

2. That believers will once again have the compassion of Jesus to practically serve the hurting and share the Gospel with families in the community.

If believers would once again soften their hearts, humble themselves to see these two realities and pray, God's Word says in 2 Chronicles 7:17, "If my people, who are called by my name, will humble themselves and pray and seek my face and turn from their wicked ways, then will I hear from heaven and will forgive their sin and will heal their land."

There are always those in each generation who have a heart for sharing God's heart with others in each generation. Will you be one of those?

Don't we want Jesus to heal those who are hurting in our land? God says He will do this, but He says that it requires humility. And in our modern, fast-paced society, that's exactly what many don't have. Since many families are in a hurry to get their own needs met, like Terry from chapter one, families typically do not have time for anyone but themselves. And sadly, it seems the more prosperous a nation is, the less sensitive the believers are to those who are hurting. We need to pray for the local church around the world to soften their hearts to the reality of hurting families who need outreach. Many have become hardened in their hearts, set in their ways, and have turned a deaf ear to those who are in need of an outreach visit. Let's not be stubborn any longer, but truly love others like Jesus loved and demonstrated throughout His life, which is, "to seek and to save the lost" (Luke 19:10 ESV).

A SIMPLE PRAYER—A SIMPLE BREAKTHROUGH

Maybe if you were honest, you would actually admit, "Brother Anthony, I can see how I have been a little bit selfish and stubborn about stepping out for Jesus. What can I do to change that?" I would then reply, "Friend, you are already on your first step in the right direction."

The first step is being humble enough to acknowledge the problem. The next step is to pray, like we are instructed in 2 Chronicles 7:14, which paraphrased says, "… Ask Jesus to forgive you." He says in His Word, "[He] will not reject a broken and repentant heart" (Psalm 51:17 NLT). He also says that when we ask for forgiveness, "There is therefore now no condemnation for those who are in Christ Jesus" (Rom. 8:1 ESV). This means you don't have to feel ashamed in any way.

Allow me to lead you in a prayer to pray aloud that will help you see a turn around in this area. Feel free to change it, anyway you want, that makes it more meaningful to you before God:

> Jesus, forgive me for resisting Your leading to share You with hurting people in the community. Also, please forgive me for not demonstrating diligence to disciple others like Your Word instructs. Please help me to overcome all fear, stubbornness, selfishness, and busyness that has hindered me from obeying Your Word in these areas. I humbly repent and ask You to help me fulfill these two

assignments, of outreach and discipleship, which You have given me through Your Word. Thank you, Jesus. I love You. And I surrender my control to the Holy Spirit for Your glory.

Now, if you prayed those words from your heart, you have prayed a very bold prayer.

WHAT NOW?

An interesting story in the Bible of what true repentance looks like is found in the story of Zacchaeus. He was desperate to see Jesus. So he climbed up a tree to watch Him. After he saw Him and heard what Jesus had to say, his immediate inner response was to give. He said, "Look, Lord! Here and now I give half of my possessions to the poor, and if I have cheated anybody out of anything, I will pay back four times the amount" (Luke 19:8 NIV). His words were not empty words. They were packed with action.

I pray that your sincere choice to ask God to forgive you and to help you is now also reflected in your daily life. You will never fail when your heart is to see people blessed, touched, and reached with the love of Jesus. God will not let you fail. How can you be so sure? It's because Scripture says, "LOVE NEVER FAILS" (1 Cor. 13:8 NIV).

Chapter 3

FAMILY FOCUS

When I first got saved, I would leave Gospel tracts everywhere. Restaurants, restrooms, even waiting rooms. You name it. Some people in my family couldn't stand it. I always felt like they looked down on me. They saw my choice to do the "ministry thing" as "copping out." They thought I should have been a respectable doctor like my dad is. Whenever I would witness and leave tracks, they would say, "Don't leave those things around when we are around ... can't you do that when you are by yourself ... that's so embarrassing." They would act completely flabbergasted, as if I was doing something that is perceived as totally socially awkward. Because of their strong influence, and just being a baby Christian at the time, I would actually question if what I was doing was appropriate or not.

Even Jesus had problems with His family. In the middle of His preaching, his family let it be known that they wanted to speak to Him. It must not have mattered to them that they were interrupting what God the Father had Him doing at the time. It says in Matthew 12:46, "While Jesus was still talking to the crowd, his mother and brothers stood outside, wanting to speak to him. Someone told him, 'Your mother and brothers are standing outside, wanting to speak to you'" (NIV).

The only place it says in the Bible that Jesus could not do any mighty work was in his hometown among his family and friends. Many times, it seems like our spiritual gifts, ministry, and the things we do for God are totally disregarded and not honored among those who know us the best. That's how it was for Jesus, too. It states in Mark 6:4, "Jesus said to them, 'Only in his hometown, among his relatives and in his own house is a prophet without honor.' He could not do any miracles there, except lay his hands on a few sick people and heal them. And he was amazed at their lack of faith" (NIV).

For many people, when they answer the call of God, they are soon to realize that their family and friends may be their toughest mission field. Though many believers are blessed with godly families, those who are not find that this could be their most difficult struggle. At such times, it's important to remember the promises for your own family's salvation in Scripture to encourage us. For instance, "Believe in the Lord Jesus, and you will be saved—you and your household" (Acts 16:31 NIV). Though our families and friends can seem like the most challenging mission field, we can always trust Jesus to guide us, empower us, and sustain us in our initiative to lead them to salvation. Our first step in reaching our lost relatives and friends is prayer.

We can pray for …

- God to show us who in our family He wants us to focus on.
- God to identify friends or co-workers He wants us to focus on.
- Whatever prayer requests that our friends and family members may have.
- Jesus to open up the opportunities for friends and family members to receive Him.
- The Holy Spirit to show us how we can be a blessing and do things that will touch their hearts to open them up to Jesus.
- The Holy Spirit to show us the best time to schedule visits to see them, pray with them, and bring a blessing for them.
- The Holy Spirit to minister to our friends and family members and bring them to a place of being born-again, their salvation through Christ.

SEEKING THE HOLY SPIRIT'S STRATEGY

The next step, once we have prayed for those who we care about, is to record that information in the Adopt-A-Family "Family Info" handbook. When you turn to the section called, "Family Focus," you will find a section to record prayer requests, contact information, areas of struggle, and a schedule for planning visits. Make sure you diligently record the information you receive from God through prayer. It is necessary to be a good steward of what the Lord reveals to you on how He wants you to minister to others.

A unique approach of the Adopt-A-Family Follow-Up format is that it is based upon servanthood. You may have heard the old saying, "Talk is cheap." Many people in our world, at least in America, have left the Church because of bad experiences with Christians or the Church. Because of the connotation that is placed on many Christians, whether they deserve it or not, it is a reality that we have to overcome. Many will say that "They don't have a problem with Jesus; they just have a problem with Christians." The only way to overcome this barrier is by praying and asking the Holy Spirit to give us supernatural strategies and grace to dismantle these kinds of hindrances, so that we can share Jesus with them.

One way the Holy Spirit can speak to us is to show us acts of service that we can do for our family and friends that will soften their hearts to open them up to receive Jesus.

As we seek the Holy Spirit on behalf of our lost family members, friends, and co-workers, we should also be ready for Him to show us prayer points that will help us pray against hindrances that are blinding them from receiving Jesus. Be sure to record both kinds of information in your "Family Info" handbook.

SERVING TO REVEAL JESUS

In the Book of James it says, "What good is it, my

brothers, if a man claims to have faith but has no deeds? Can such faith save him? Suppose a brother or sister is without clothes and daily food. If one of you says to him, 'Go, I wish you well; keep warm and well fed,' but does nothing about his physical needs, what good is it" (2:14 NIV).

Scripture teaches us that we are supposed to offer a service to those who are hurting, and not just pass them by, as the Levite did, who paid no attention to the needs of his neighbor in Luke 10:32. Jesus illustrated through this story the obligation we have as Christians to be a true neighbor, to our friends and family, and to reveal Jesus to them by demonstrating it through loving service—even as He served us. In doing so, it will show lost families in the community that we are different from any other Christians that they have ever encountered.

When we reflect that we are true Christians through our actions and not just our words, we earn the right to be a voice in their lives. They may have had many other Christians preach to them, and give them truth, but they never had a believer demonstrate what the love of Jesus looks like through tangible service. That's our job as followers of Jesus, to imitate this model of serving and to be a blessing to those who are hurting. In doing so, we will have an open door to share Jesus with them. Providing for them through an act of loving service will dismantle every wall.

Jesus Himself modeled this in Matthew 15:32, "Jesus called his disciples to him and said, 'I have compassion for these people; they have already been with me three days and have nothing to eat. I do not want to send them away hungry, or they may collapse on the way.'" His ministry went beyond just miracles, preaching, and teaching. His love was so great for mankind that He even chose to minister to our human needs to show us how much He truly cares. As He was, so should we be. We should live to imitate Him.

A story I'll never forget as a student at Christ For The Nations Institute, is when I felt a burden come on me during my devotional time. It was Isaiah 58:6, which says:

"Is not this the kind of fasting I have chosen: to loose the chains of injustice and untie the cords of the yoke, to set the oppressed free and break every yoke? Is it not to share your food with the hungry and to provide the poor wanderer with shelter—when you see the naked, to clothe them, and not to turn away from your own flesh and blood?" (NIV).

When I was reading this Scripture one day, a thought came to me. I had never done both at the same time. I had never fasted and gone out to feed the hurting at the same time in order to share Jesus. I honestly felt convicted. So convicted in fact, that I felt if I didn't fast and go out and feed the homeless that day for lunch, I honestly thought I was going to miss God. I had never gone out to feed the homeless up until that point. Not knowing where to go, I called up Virginia, my friend, who had plenty of homeless ministry experience in Dallas. I asked her, "Do you know where to find the homeless in Dallas?"

She responded by telling me of an intersection where I could find them. She also said that she would join me.

So, in blind faith, I prepared some sandwiches and put them in plastic baggies. Then I drove up to the parking lot across the street from the homeless shelter. This area seemed to be like a homeless city. Streams of people, dressed in rags, were going into and from out of this giant, dilapidated building that looked like an old library. Inside, what appeared to be their gates of shelter, there were mounds of trash and makeshift barbecue grills. Tin cans were tossed everywhere. Keep in mind that I was convicted to do this while I was fasting.

When we pulled up, we parked in front of a fence that circled the parking lot. All along the perimeter were hurting people, walking alongside the fence. Right when we pulled out the cooler from the truck, instantly those who were walking by began to wave at us, saying, "Hey, over here! ... Can you help me out Ma'am?"

Without even having a chance to completely unload, we found ourselves handing out sandwiches over the fence. We were also rapidly asking them, before they walked off, if we could pray for them. Some would stop and even put their hands through the fence, so we could join our hands with them while we prayed.

They seemed so receptive to prayer that even Virginia and I were moved to tears as we were praying with them. Something about doing this, while I was fasting, made it feel so real and even extra powerful. This is only my opinion, but it was an amazing experience.

Of all those who walked by and took a sandwich, there was only one man who declined. When he started to walk by us, I extended a sandwich to him. Initially, he reached his hand out toward it like he was going to take it. Then he withdrew his hand and said, "Nah, I don't want your sandwich." Then, he turned and walked away.

ONLY ONE MAN DIDN'T WANT A SANDWICH

A little bit grieved by the man's response, I just watched him walk away. I couldn't help but wonder what he had been through to make him so irritated. I learned later that this man had been evacuated from New Orleans during the catastrophic hurricane disaster called Katrina.

As we kept praying for the others and blessing people with sandwiches, the man who had first walked off, was now back. He said, "I'll take your sandwich," and then quickly grabbed it out of my hand. Then, with much intensity and conviction, he said, "Earlier today, I saw a vision of a wall of fire and two people had their hands reaching inside of it. As they would reach inside this wall of fire, they would pull people out, and the people would fall to their knees behind them, and worship a great light that was protecting them from behind. When I walked by and I saw you two praying for people through the fence, this is what it reminded me of."

Not knowing completely what to think, I figured that it was the Holy Spirit who was drawing this man.

I offered him prayer. He accepted. I then said to him, "Sir, can I take you to Golden Corral to buy you a buffet meal and take you to the Tuesday Night Experience service at Christ For The Nations Institute tonight?" He said, "Yes." That night, after the service, James went up to the altar, curled up like a child, and bawled his eyes out. As the power of God touched him, He said it felt as if the Father was holding him in His arms.

The complete story of the friendship that James and I had after that is another book. However, I will say that to this day James and I are still friends. I learned later that he had been diagnosed with HIV. Around five years after I met James, as a student at Christ For The Nations Institute, he received a doctor's report that he was now no longer HIV positive. He also has gotten a job and is working for a rehabilitation home to help those who want to come out of the street life. God has also opened up doors for him to speak. Since that time, he has traveled to tell his story in different Christian venues around the United States. Whenever James and I get together, from time-to-time, he nonchalantly says to me, "Do you remember this all started with just a sandwich?"

It is only the Holy Spirit who can give us the courage to lay down our pride, our self-centeredness, and our busyness, to slow down and serve a hurting brother—or a hurting family. It's in those moments ... we most look like Jesus. I give all the glory to Him for this testimony and all the other testimonies like it. It wasn't that the sandwich was powerful or holy in and of itself, it wasn't that there was anything special about my incidental obedience, it was that it created an opportunity for the Holy Spirit to touch a life.

This is what I am talking about. Anybody can do this. Using what Jesus said to do works for anybody. Like I said in chapter two, it's just a matter of how much we are willing to cooperate with the Holy Spirit that determines how many of these kinds of stories we will have in our lives—yes, even on Judgment Day.

ADOPT-A-FAMILY IS SIMPLE

The Adopt-A-Family Follow-Up format is simple. It is based upon a few biblical principles:

1. Pray and ask the Holy Spirit how to best bless or serve someone in your family, friends, or community. Ask Him when to do it.

2. Visit them to deliver the blessing or service, as the Lord leads you.

3. Upon visiting them, pray with them and read a Scripture with them. Offer to bring them another blessing for a "Return Visit" next week, and record the date and time in your "Family Info" handbook Also, utilize the "Return Visit" card and "First Touch" cards to be organized about the follow-up.

4. Repeat steps 1 through 3 indefinitely, as long as the Lord leads you.

Congratulations, you are now discipling someone! You are now doing what Jesus said when He commanded, "Teaching them to obey all that I have commanded you" (Matthew 28:20 NIV).

James and I had many more experiences together since that initial encounter, which I believe changed both of our lives. It involved me taking time to serve and bless him on multiple occasions that did not necessarily benefit me in anyway. Maybe some would have called that investment into a homeless person's life foolish, but I wouldn't trade it for a ton of gold. I gained a friend. And because of the moments we spent together as result of me making time for him, he had plenty of time to learn about Jesus, the gospel message, and to receive it wholeheartedly.

This is the hope of the Adopt-A-Family Follow-Up format, that the Holy Spirit would empower people to serve and build long-lasting relationships with hurting families, so that those who need more than just a drive-by Gospel message would have plenty of opportunities to receive Jesus over a long-lasting relationship.

Chapter 4

FIRST TOUCH

I remember when I first got saved. I was so recklessly willing to step out on a limb to do anything for Jesus. My zeal was plentiful, but my wisdom was still growing. The idea of one-on-one witnessing was quite a mystical thing to me at that time, but nonetheless captivating. That risky adventure of talking to strangers seemed like a great unknown that I was itching to delve into.

Once I received some teaching on evangelism, the first encounter I had was in the park with a man named Kevin. He was actually drinking a beer at the time. My friend and I, while driving by the park, saw him sitting at a picnic table. For some reason, we felt drawn to him. So we turned the car around and parked. We walked across the lawn ever so gleefully, thoroughly expecting the Lord to do what only He can do. I am sure we seemed a little goofy and awkward to the man as we approached him, but we were determined.

Needless to say, Kevin accepted the Lord. What we experienced that day isn't some strange occurrence, nor is it for just a few believers. We are all called to be witnesses. Anyone can effectively bridge the gap between witnessing and discipleship. Just as I, in the beginning, did not know what to expect, and even felt nervous, I let my expectation in God override my fears.

Whenever you approach someone to share the Gospel with, always focus on the positive outcome—the Lord is the One Who is doing it. It may feel awkward to some degree to our human nature to step-out and do something by faith. The element of risk and choosing to allow your trust to be placed in an invisible God for positive results puts our flesh in a place of discomfort that only the Holy Spirit can guide us through. Our flesh will most definitely try to scream in defiance. Our complete reliance on the Holy Spirit in those moments is our greatest key, and the results are more rewarding than words can express.

In the coziness of our Christian circles, sometimes we neglect to pay attention to those who are fatherless and without families in the world. Psalm 68:6 says, "God sets the lonely in families" and that He is "A father to the fatherless" (NIV). Just by opening our hearts to those who are in our daily paths, we can be part of God's plan to introduce the hurting to the family of God.

Visiting homes is a great way to reach families or those who are hurting. Whether they live in an apartment complex, or a nice suburban home, if you knock on a neighborhood door, you are sure to meet someone who will need to know about Jesus. The first step when meeting someone at the door or on the street is to simply greet them and introduce yourself. When you are warm to strangers, you will find that they will reciprocate the kindness. Love can be tangibly felt. *Explain to them that you are from the church, and you are here in the area to be a blessing in the community.*

In my evangelism manual, *The American Mission: Soulwinner's Manual*, I go into great detail on how to witness, and I highly recommend it as a companion reading resource to this manual. For the purposes of this book, I keep the witnessing element of teaching relatively basic. Below is an effective guideline to follow.

Step 1: The Greeting

After sharing with them who you are and why you are in the area, you can ask them if you can pray for them. You will see their hearts melt and open up as you share the love of Christ with them by blessing them with prayer. If they respond with they can't think of anything for you to pray for, just ask them if you can pray to bless their home and family. You will notice a softness and receptivity in their countenance after you pray for them.

Step 2: Share Jesus

This is the ideal time to begin sharing a short, 3 minute testimony of how Jesus saved you. In doing so, you will be able to communicate a heartfelt witness for Jesus. After sharing with them the story of Jesus and how someone can be saved, you can then ask them, "If you are serious about getting your life right with God, I would be glad to lead you in a prayer to receive Jesus

Christ as your Lord and Savior. Would you like to do that now?" Regardless of whether they say yes or no and receive Jesus at this time, it's important that we stay in touch with this family, which brings us to our next step.

Step 3: Adopt-A-Family Follow-Up

The Adopt-A-Family follow-up format is meant to bridge the gap between the outreach and discipleship. Once you have made your sincere attempt to share Jesus with a family in the community, now it is time to utilize the "First Touch" follow-up card and ask the following four questions.

1. How are you doing on groceries? Could you use some?
2. What time would be the best time to bring you those groceries if not this time next week?
3. Would you like to come to our church sometime?
4. Would you like it if we saved you some money on gas and picked you up tomorrow for our service at 9:30 a.m.?

Remember: Adjust the pick-up time to be 15-30 minutes before the start of the main morning service.

Also, groceries are offered for the purpose of this example. However, other services may be adapted for each demographic according to the information in the chapter, "Adapting the Vision."

Step 4: Record the Responses

Once you have asked these four questions, circle the yes or no options on the "First Touch" card, according to their answers, and fill in the "Return Visit" time in entry #2. Of course, it will be very important to document any follow-up contact information for future communication with this family. This information will be crucial for setting up future services, including prayer times, rides to church, and prayer over the phone as the relationship grows. A comfortable and natural way to inquire this information is to ask,

"If there happened to be a change in the delivery of the groceries [or other services], can we get your contact information to call you if we need to make adjustments?"

Also, be sure to ask them for permission for the church to contact them in the future.

Step 5: Copy Info into the Adopt-A-Family "Family Info" Handbook

When they have shared their information with you, then record it in the corresponding spaces provided on the "First Touch" card. After the outreach, be sure to record that information into your Adopt-A-Family "Family Info" Handbook for your personal reference. Also, be sure to deliver all of the "First Touch" cards to the Outreach Coordinator for the church records at the end of the outreach.

After these five steps are completed, the next step will be the "Return Visit," which is discussed in the next chapter. Ideally, at least one member from the original group who initially ministered to the family should be a part of every "Return Visit." However, if none are available, the Outreach Coordinator may choose a couple of church family members to substitute for the "Return Visit" on a case-by-case basis. In order to build a strong relational bridge between the church family and the families in the community, at least one family member in the initial visit needs to take the responsibility to be faithful to attend each "Return Visit." The family in the community will feel most comfortable with visiting and possibly joining the church family because of the faithful visit of a few church family members.

Though my encounter with meeting Kevin on a park bench was years back, it really does seem like it only happened yesterday. After we talked to him for a while, I shared my testimony with him. I explained how I went from being a Catholic, to an atheist, to a spirit-filled follower of Jesus. Kevin surprisingly wanted to get born-again.

Truthfully, my buddy and I were both kind of shocked. This was the first salvation I had ever seen as a Christian. Even though Kevin was roughly 13 years older than me, he allowed me to continue to pick him up for church from that day forward.

Another interesting factor here is I was just a baby-Christian myself. I'd only been saved for about 2 years at this time, but God used me to disciple Kevin for about two years. To this day, Kevin still calls me and expresses his gratitude to me for taking the time to be a positive Christian friend in his life.

This is the joy of discipling someone who has come out of a hurting lifestyle. The beautiful thing is seeing the person you used to know as a lost-stranger now answering the call of God. It is also rewarding to watch how the Holy Spirit transforms his or her life. There are no words to describe the inner satisfaction that comes along with allowing the Holy Spirit to move through you in this way. In manifesting the words of Jesus Who said, "Go therefore and make disciples of all nations, baptizing them in the name of the Father and of the Son and of the Holy Spirit" (Matthew 28:19 ESV).

This was His plan; this is our plan.

Chapter 5

THE RETURN VISIT

One of the most life-changing stories I remember from the Evangelism Student Ministry at Christ For The Nations, was when the team came out to help me minister for a church in Grand Prairie, Texas. During the teaching sessions, while we were on an outreach with members from the church and CFNI students present, God mightily began to empower the students and church members.

After the healing teaching, a young woman from CFNI, named Laura, said she had had persistent back pain since she was a girl. So I led the church members to sit her down in a chair and measure the length of her legs. One leg was very significantly longer than the other. Doctors will tell you that many times back pain is exacerbated by a short leg, and this condition is more common than people think.

As I taught the church family members to operate in the power of God, Laura said she felt an intense electric-like power run throughout her body. Church members began to "ooh and aww," as they watched her leg grow to the same length as her other leg. Now they were equal. She also said she felt that electric-like power moving through her back, aligning her vertebrae.

Apart from what those who witnessed it first-hand will

tell you, below is her hand-written testimony:

> "Anthony was preaching an instructional message on faith and healing before we went out … So Anthony began to pray for me with my legs still stretched out. The power of God fell on me immediately, until my whole body was shaking …Suddenly, Andrew, one who previously got healed, gasped and remarked that he was watching my leg stretch out to meet the other leg, as God reformed my back. Since then, my back has been completely delivered from pain."
>
> -Laura, CFNI Student

If that wasn't wild enough, she said she felt that same electric-like power from God running throughout her body for the duration of that afternoon outreach, and her bones continued to move. By the end of the outreach, she testified and gave glory to God for how He completely healed her in the course of a couple of hours. All of the glory be to Jesus!

Also, at the end of the outreach, the Evangelism Student Leader at that time, Gabe, testified about how the church outreach had been so fruitful. He told the story of how he and a couple of students with a church member were invited to go inside a family's apartment. As they sat-down, they found themselves in the living room with a man who was over six foot tall, dressed in camouflage, sitting in a big chair. He said that initially they were a little bit intimidated by this massive man, though strangely enough, he seemed to be quite inquisitive. When they initiated some friendly conversation, they asked him about what he believed. He told them he was Mormon. Respectfully, the team began talking about Jesus and the Bible. Then they asked him if he would like for them to come back in the future and teach him about the Bible. Tears welled up in his eyes; he said, "Yes, please come back."

It is in moments like these, we learn the awesome power of follow-up. Imagine how many families in the community today, sit and wait for someone to come and bring them hope. We must never harden our hearts to the effectiveness of discipleship and long-term relationships with hurting families.

Jesus said, "The King will reply, 'I tell you the truth, whatever you did for one of the least of these brothers of mine, you did for me'" (Matthew 25:40 NIV). Whenever we choose to obey the Gospel and be an extension of God's family to those who are hurting, down and out, and considered lowly, that is actually how we are treating Jesus. Jesus will not let us go unrewarded on that Day. Though sometimes we may perceive it as a momentary inconvenience to share Jesus, the reward we experience in eternity will far outweigh any amount of gold or silver in this life.

DELIVERING A BLESSING

The next step of the Adopt-A-Family format is this "Return Visit." This will be the second encounter that a family from the church will have with a family in the community. I will walk you through some basic and practical information on what to do during this visit. One of the reasons why the family you are focusing on in the community will be excited about your Return Visit is because you are coming with a blessing from the church for them. The default blessing will likely be groceries, unless you have been directed otherwise by a decision from the Outreach Coordinator.

For the sake of the format to be financially feasible for church families to be sustained long-term, I suggest that no more than $5-7 dollars worth of groceries be delivered. For example, you can buy a dozen eggs, a half-gallon of milk, and a loaf of bread for this price. You may have to purchase the generic brand from the grocery store or buy from a dollar store, but it is possible. Also, I suggest that you do not change the items as much as possible, for the sake of not raising their expectations. Many times, the enemy will try to bring division through subtle disappointments that may creep in because of different items rendered. It's best to avoid these incidents and stick with nearly identical items, if possible.

The goal is to be a blessing, while also keeping the relationship from being compromised. This also protects the visiting family from being sucked into having to deliver more and more items, which may alter the nature of the relationship, instead of being more grocery-centered than Christ-centered. However, further assistance can be available for the family as I present in the next paragraph.

FURTHER ASSISTANCE

Unfortunately, only Jesus can actually be their provider because of His unlimited resources. If the person desires additional help, besides the $5-7 dollar limit, let them know that this is possible, but this requires them to come to church and talk to the senior pastor about it after the service. This way you are not denying them, but you are deferring them to your senior pastor, who will know best how to accommodate them with wisdom. Using this approach keeps the visiting family protected in a number of ways. The visiting family should not feel any pressure to deliver more than what has been prescribed by the Outreach Coordinator.

If the families are not able to provide the blessing out of their own pocket, I recommend for the Church to do an occasional Outreach Community Offering or create a budget to cover the costs of those families who are financially not able to cover the expenses. Scripture teaches us that we should, "Give, and it will be given to you. A good measure, pressed down, shaken together and running over, will be poured into your lap. For with the measure you use, it will be measured to you" (Luke 6:38 NIV). It is not uncommon for God to move on the heart of a church member who may have a business or access to food items that will desire to support such an outreach to share the love of Jesus with people. God has an uncanny way of providing, just when we think we don't have the resources, if we will only stop and pray to ask Him.

WHAT TO TALK ABOUT

No doubt, the family is going to be excited to see you and be blessed that you remembered them. Since this is the second time you are visiting, the awkwardness of the initial visit will have greatly subsided. On this "Return Visit" you are going to want to accomplish a couple of things:

CHECKLIST:
1. Greet the Family. Love on them. Deliver the blessing of groceries.

2. Ask them how they are doing.
   • How many children do they have?
   • What are their names? Husband and wife's name?
   • Are there any struggles the church can lift them up in prayer about?
   • Record Responses on "Return Visit" Card

3. Share a short, encouraging Scripture with them and have them read it back to you. Ask them what they think about it.

4. Ask them when you can schedule the next "Return Visit" to bring groceries.

5. Offer to save them money on gas and give them a ride to church in the morning. Establish an exact pick up time, preferably 15-30 minutes before the service starts.

6. Cheerfully close with a prayer and blessing for their family and home.

After you have visited with them, you will have experienced the wonderful and fulfilling feeling of obeying the words of Jesus to His disciple. For some families to become truly committed and transformed by Jesus, it will take a long-term discipleship relationship that will help them stay encouraged. Many families have heard the Gospel, but never have had a born-again believer, of greater maturity than themselves, walk with them and teach them what it means to be a Christian.

You will witness the powerful transformation even within your own family, as you step out and obey the words of Jesus. Your own children will become more devoted to Jesus to want to help people as they see their mom and dad model discipleship in reaching their community.

Adopting a hurting family is always a win-win situation for both families. It's just like the man in the camouflage suit, who the CFNI students got to share Jesus with in an apartment complex. There are those who are hurting, and who wait for hope to come to them. You should have seen the faces of those students after that encounter. Though they seemed a little juiced up from their adrenaline rush, they exuded with excitement from having a powerful impact on someone who was hungry for Jesus.

This is the excitement and reward of those who are willing to obey the words of Jesus and disciple as He commanded us. There is no greater joy than experiencing the Holy Spirit move through you in this way to touch a life—a family.

Chapter 6

FAMILY TO FAMILY

I'll never forget the story of Leanne. She was so fearful and apprehensive about doing an outreach during a teaching series I was doing at a church in Rhome, Texas. She would say, "I hope I got it all...<fret fret> What if I don't remember something? Do I have to remember it all!?" Then I said, "Leanne, relax! I over-taught you! You don't have to remember all of that teaching for the outreach today. The material that you learned will help you the rest of your Christian life. You can just do a couple of basic things while you are at the outreach today, and still get results!" She responded with a sigh of relief.

However, it wasn't but a few moments later that I recognized her shifting eyes were again at work, indicating that the wheels upstairs had once again begun to turn. I felt a little bit sorry for her because of her nervousness, but I knew that she would be ok, once we got out on the outreach.

The story of Leanne is quite common. She could only see the front-side of the mountain and not the horizon beyond. First-time outreach participants often deal with these struggles because they are failing to see the harvest that lies ahead... the families yet to be touched by God.

The great reward of "Community Outreach" is the reality of families reaching out to families. Just as God spoke to Abraham, "All the families on earth will be blessed through you" (Genesis 12:3 NLT). We are called to be the family of believers who reaches the families of the Earth. Our ultimate goal is to bring families into the family of God.

As we have discussed in other chapters about how to handle an initial outreach visit and how to do the follow-up visit, this chapter is about practical ways of how to incorporate those families into the church family life.

The average family who struggles through life has enough reasons and distractions to fail on following through with attending church. It is up to us to be creative about ways to serve them in the midst of their valley of decision. We can do so by making it as easy as possible for them to say yes. Perhaps the most influencing force that will attract them to attend our church family is our personal consistency in our Return Visits. When we demonstrate to the families in the community how committed we are to faithfully deliver the blessing we offered to them, our local assembly will be their first choice to visit.

A simple, yet practical way, to be fruitful in inviting new-comers to church is by offering to give them a ride, in order to save them gas money. This communicates hospitality, sensitivity to their finances, and a willingness to serve them in helping them get to church. It also provides accountability for those who may forget to come on their own.

From time-to-time, a family that is being visited may

desire a greater quantity of grocery assistance. Do not look at this as an "oh no" moment. Since the Adopt-A-Family format is designed to be adaptable, affordable, and sustainable, a church member must not feel the pressure or obligation to take on such a load beyond their 5 to 7 dollar weekly delivery. Instead, kindly inform the person that "further assistance is available, but only through the senior pastor. In turn, he or she would be glad to talk to you about providing that service, after the Sunday church service."

At this point, there is no need to feel guilty because you have not denied them. You have simply given them a motivation to now meet your senior pastor and attend church. Only the senior pastor, or the Outreach Coordinator, if he or she has been given that authority, should handle such cases of additional levels of assistance beyond what's been prescribed per outreach. They will know how to best help them without saying the wrong.

MEALS THAT HEAL

Another practical tool to give local families an incentive to make this Sunday the day they choose to attend our local church, could be the appeal of an after-service church luncheon. This opportunity to bless new-coming families with a plate of food and loving fellowship could be what it takes to wet the appetite of families to attend the services. Once a family in the community has ventured out to finally attend a service, it is important to make them feel as welcomed as possible. If you see a new-coming family in the service, do not hesitate to be the kind-hearted person who takes them out for dinner after the service to make them feel like they are a part of the family.

I remember when I first got saved and started attending a church. One of the things I always looked forward to was enjoying a meal and fellowship with my church family. I can still remember to this day how strongly the family atmosphere of eating dinner with other members encouraged me. This alone was one of the reasons I wanted to keep going to church. Many families that are new need this relationship building time in order to solidify their membership in the local church. We should be the family who provides that positive fellowship experience that makes them want to come back time and time again. This is the relational glue that holds families together.

GIVE-AWAY INCENTIVE

One time, I was doing an outreach equipping series for a pastor in Harare, Zimbabwe. For seven nights straight I taught on evangelism and the power of God. The pastor said that because of the Give-away Program his church had the highest attendance he had ever seen during those meetings. The miracles that people testified of taking place during the meetings were incredible.

One miracle was a family whose daughter was delivered from witchcraft. Right in the middle of my preaching, she began to cry and yelled out, "It hurts; it hurts ... the needle in my arm." A little surprised and confused, I asked the interpreter what she was talking about. I soon realized it was witchcraft related. She stumbled along, crying to the altar. I then took authority and commanded that needle and unclean spirit attached to it that entered her arm supernaturally through witchcraft to come out in the Name of Jesus. She let out a scream and fell on the ground exasperated.

A couple of days later, she attended church again with an X-ray. She showed us how the doctors had actually identified a piece of metal that looked like a sewing needle in the core of her arm from before the service. She then testified that the needle had left her arm for the glory of Jesus that night.

This young girl was set free because of the willingness of church members to bring her to church. A witchcraft phenomenon like this is very common in Africa. Of course we give all the glory to Jesus for His Name being greater than any power of the enemy. This is just one of the supernatural ways God can touch visitors, like Jesus did in the gospels, by casting out unclean spirits. The most common challenge, however, is not casting out the spirits, but getting those who need deliverance to show up in the first place.

Here are some practical ways to increase the attendance of a church service evangelistically:

    A. Offer incentives and motivate families in the
       Church to invite guests to a service by doing
       a raffle where church members can win prizes

after the service. Inform the church members that for each guest they bring, his or her name will be entered into a drawing for prizes an additional time. Reward the church members at the end of the service with the prizes. Usually, church members enjoy the excitement of being seen as "the winner." This encourages families in the church to bring multiple members, and it creates a little friendly competition for a godly purpose of bringing people to Church.

B. Empower church members to be more successful in inviting guests by doing a raffle for all newcomers. The give-away may increase the appeal of family and friends to attend church. Enter each visitor's name into a drawing for a chance to win gift cards, mp3 players, iPads, burrito cards, ice cream cards, or other popular items. Distribute the prizes at the end of service. This could be considered "fishing bait," which is meant to help church members become better "fisher's of men" (Mark 1:17 ESV). Through being a blessing to potential newcomers, this opens the door to share Jesus with them.

SOME TIPS ON CONDUCTING GIVE-AWAYS:

A. Opt to give away many small items, so that there are many winners.
B. Great gift cards that get people's attention are Best Buy, Amazon, Chic-fil-A, and Walmart.
C. Gift card amounts don't necessarily need to be large in order to be effective.
D. Larger prizes like iPads, Ipods, and Tablet PCs can create a major buzz and participation.
E. Advertise and Promote the give-away inside and outside of the church.
F. Make it fun!
G. Do it prayerfully and ask the Holy Spirit for guidance.

One of the most important ways a give-away can be an effective tool for reaching new families is that it can provide an opportunity for you to collect follow-up information. For each new family that attends a service which incorporates a give-away, it is wise to have them fill out their contact information on the drawing slip. This allows you to be able to stay in touch with them in the future.

Later on, the Outreach Coordinator or someone from the church may feel led to call that family and pray with them or invite them to come to church again, or schedule a "Return Visit." It is also suggested to include a little check box on the slip that says, "I give the church permission to contact me in the future." Such families may also be interested in receiving an Adopt-A-Family grocery service that would enable the church family to cultivate a long-term discipleship relationship with them.

When you step out to be a blessing to a family, you will always be pleasantly surprised with the results. I remember the story of Leanne and what happened to her on an outreach. She knocked on the door, and an old woman answered, using a walker. Feeling quite nervous, she asked her if she could pray for her. She said, "Yes." When Leanne prayed, the woman all of a sudden felt energized. She said that she felt like fire had gone from the top of her head to the tip of her toes. She also yelped, "I feel my legs strengthening." Miraculously, she immediately set aside her walker and stood straight up, without any assistance. Leanne was astonished.

Afterwards, the woman told Leanne that she could not drive because of her legs. However, after she had been prayed for and received her healing, she drove herself to church that night and shared her testimony. She even brought a friend.

Isn't it wonderful how God chooses to use us to bring families into the house of God? It's always for His glory and only by the power of the Holy Spirit moving through us—there is no greater joy. In doing so, we bring pleasure to God, for it is written, "And without faith it is impossible to please God" (Hebrews 11:6 NIV).

Chapter 7

THE OUTREACH COORDINATOR

Homeless people were shouting. Some of them were saying, "Amen," some of them were jeering. They formed a line that went down the block and around the corner—such a river of people, all eagerly awaiting their distribution. Standing on a stepladder, with Christ For The Nations students, who were standing behind me and in front of me, I boldly articulated my testimony through a mobile speaker and a mic from across the street. I could see across the road that students were engaging with people that looked like they were dressed in rags. Some of the students had their hands on the shoulders of those waiting in line, praying for them. The combination of the one-on-one ministry and the salvation testimonies of students from different nations filling the airways through the PA system was a sight to behold.

Of all the things that I learned in my four years of Bible school, arguably the most transformational times of my life were when I was the student leader of the evangelism ministry at Christ For The Nations Institute. The job of organizing, administrating, and cultivating a team of leaders that would co-labor in the harvest underneath my authority, taught me responsibility and skills that I am still using to this day. The responsibility of maintaining and inspiring the task of evangelism was not an easy task.

My background is not Pentecostal, protestant, or even that of evangelical faith. I never even heard that Christians were supposed to read the Bible regularly and practice it, until I was around 20-years-old. As far as Christianity goes, I was exclusively familiar with Catholic traditions and the saints, but that was it.

In high school, I became an atheist. When I got saved after being an atheist, I felt a deep move in my heart to discover the Bible. In the midst of my innocent study of God's Word, I found Scriptures that were not practiced in my local church. A longing in my heart resounded to do something for God's Kingdom. Sadly, however, my corresponding discovery was that all the ministry positions seemed to be taken in the Church. Not seeing an opening for a senior pastor, Sunday school teacher, youth pastor, or office secretary, was quite disconcerting to me.

However, hope arose in me after a careful study of God's Word. To my excitement, I found a role in my Bible that I saw no one in my church filling. These were my first two thoughts. If no one in the church is doing it, then that means it's a legitimate need. And the second was, if no one is doing it, then that means no one can tell me that I am doing it the wrong way. The Scripture I found was Ephesians 4:11-13.

> "And he gave the apostles, the prophets, the
> evangelists, the shepherds and teachers, to equip
> the saints for the work of ministry, for building

up the body of Christ, until we all attain to the unity of the faith and of the knowledge of the Son of God, to mature manhood, to the measure of the stature of the fullness of Christ, …"

Even as a baby Christian, God gave me this revelation that the job of an evangelist was for the local church, to equip the saints. Immediately, after this epiphany, I grabbed all the Chick tracts off my church wall and got to work. With blind zeal, I did not hesitate to set off to the local college campus to share the Gospel.

Practically speaking, the role of an evangelist in the local church setting can be purely extracted from Scripture. Below, I have included 6 bullet points of what the job of an evangelist in the local church entails:

- Organizes Outreaches
- Cultivates a Team of Co-Leaders
- Submits and Serves the Vision of the Senior Pastor
- Oversees Follow-Up
- Encourages the Body to Celebrate Outreaches and Discipleship
- Equips the Body of Christ to do the same

Just as the five-fold ministry that is ordained in Ephesians 4:11 gives a leadership structure and departmental function for each member of the five-fold ministry, the evangelist provides leadership in that particular area. Romans 13:1 says," For there is no authority except from God, and those that exist have been instituted by God." As the senior pastor provides leadership over the local church body in a general sense, the evangelist serves as a delegated authority under submission to the pastor. In doing so, both offices are able to do their job more effectively as a ministry team. The ministry of the evangelist bears fruit that is long-lasting because of it working in God's ordained authority, structured through the local church. Consequently, the senior pastor enjoys the benefits of a growing church related to properly maintained outreaches.

A properly operating five-fold ministry team results in a win-win situation for the whole Body of Christ because the responsibilities are properly delegated so that no one member suffers the burn-out of carrying all of the load. Jesus is the only One Who gets to choose how He wants His Church authority and delegated structure to be set up. The local church that does not honor Jesus' word, regarding the five-fold ministry, will find themselves not producing the fruit that Jesus has called them to produce.

When I got started doing the work of an evangelist, all I had to go on was zeal. Over time, my zeal was refined into maturity through learning from my experiences and mentors. Every young person who feels the call of an evangelist should have a mentor. However, mentor or not, don't let anything stop you from doing what God has put in your heart.

An Outreach Coordinator will need some things to be

successful. The functions suggested below are given that the church leadership has made a decision to incorporate an Outreach Coordinator or a variation thereof:

- Church Support and Participation
- Outreach Resources: Portable Sound System, Mobile Stages, Clothes, Other Give-away Items
- Outreach Promotional Materials: Posters, E-Mail Broadcasts, Social Media Announcements
- Sunday Morning Outreach Testimonies and Outreach Announcements
- Administration Tools

In the next chapter, I will present how to be an Outreach Coordinator. When I had the privilege and honor of leading and teaching students how to share their faith, while I was in Bible School, I'll never forget the story of Annie. She was such a shy and prayerful young-lady. She was totally unassuming when it came to someone who would step out boldly in faith. I looked at her during an outreach and said, "Do you want to street-preach?" And she timidly, said, "Really?" I said, "Yes, you can do it." She responded with trepidation, "How?" I said, "It's easy; all you have to do is start preaching your testimony, and God will guide you from there. The Gospel will start coming out of your mouth naturally."

So, I'll never forget the day when Annie took me seriously and stood up in front of a mass of homeless people and declared her testimony. It was powerful how she glorified Christ. She is still preaching around the world today.

This is the kind of rewarding experience that one can look forward to as an Outreach Coordinator. It is the reward of seeing those whom you have worked with, diligently, step into their God given call, or at least move to another level because of the Holy Spirit moving through you. Any leadership task God entrusts us with is always all for His glory, empowered by His Spirit, and for His will and His will alone.

Chapter 8

HOW TO BE AN OUTREACH COORDINATOR

Dr. John Maxwell says, "Everything rises and falls on leadership." Though the joys and rewards of leading are many, the costs are also many. I'll never forget what happened to me at a time when I was younger in the Lord. A pastor I was submitted to expressed some discontentment with me. As I sat in his baseball and sports memorabilia-filled office, he said, "When are you going to take care of 'home?' This is your church. What are you doing to help it?"

At that time, God had really begun to open up doors for me to minister around the nation. In my mind, I was thinking, what does he mean? "Doesn't he know I'm already ministering?" A little bit taken back by his words, he went on to say, "What about our website; the college and career group doesn't have a website." Again, I was thinking, "Why does he need me to do a website? I'm not a web-designer; I'm an evangelist." I also thought, "I'm too busy to do that."

Somehow I felt convicted. So, reluctantly, I said, "Ok." My response wasn't exactly exuberant, but I did make the choice to respect my senior pastor. I got to work building a website for the college and career group. It was a humbling and time-consuming experience—one that I honestly did not see how it could ever benefit me personally, but I did it because I loved my pastor.

Eventually, my pastor became pleased with my work. Not long after, I was promoted to be one of the college and career group core team leaders. Even though the website was very time-consuming, and in my mind I thought I could be committing my time to something else that benefits me, God ended up rewarding me for my faithfulness. Scripture teaches us that, "Whoever can be trusted with very little can also be trusted with much, and whoever is dishonest with very little will also be dishonest with much" (Luke 16:10 NIV).

Our ultimate model and example of leadership is Jesus. Jesus demonstrated through His life and teaching that, "The greatest among you will be your servant" (Matthew 23:11 NIV). Our vision and heart for leadership should be with the motive of serving people and meeting their needs, instead of our own. Sometimes, this does not make sense, especially when we are young and ambitious in the Lord, but the Holy Spirit grows us to be more like Jesus, in this way, as we mature in the Lord. We must always accept any assignment the Holy Spirit gives us, regardless of how much we may or may not want to do it. All leadership is birthed, initiated, empowered, and led along by the Holy Spirit for His purposes alone, and many times, this can be a humbling experience.

In the last chapter, we discussed what an Outreach

Coordinator does. Though the title and terminology can change from church to church, the basic function of the Outreach Coordinator will stay relatively the same. In this chapter, I will explain how an Outreach Coordinator serves the Body of Christ and provides leadership in specific areas. Whether or not one feels called to be an Outreach Coordinator, to learn about this ministry can benefit any Christian's walk.

In order to be an Outreach Coordinator, you will need to know your tools. Each tool is significant and important to being effective. Keep in mind, as we discussed in the last chapter, an Outreach Coordinator will need to learn the basic skills to carry out the following tasks:

- Organize Outreaches
- Cultivate a Team of Co-Leaders
- Submit to and Serve the Vision of the Senior Pastor
- Oversee all Follow-Up
- Encourage the Body to Celebrate Outreaches and Discipleship
- Equip the Body of Christ to do the same

ORGANIZES OUTREACHES

Perhaps the most obvious function of an Outreach Coordinator is to steward consistent outreaches. Unless outreaches are consistent, then one will also discover that people's attendance is also inconsistent. Consistency is the key ingredient in order to build the discipline of church-goers to make outreaches a part of their everyday life. Consistent outreach participation can be cultivated in the following ways:

A. Putting up posters and passing out flyers will keep the people informed about the dates and times the outreaches are taking place. A free sample poster is available at www.anthonydee.com/resources in a free downloadable Adopt-A-Family Starter packet.

B. Announcements during services to inform the people of God about when the outreaches are planned. Keep in mind, this should only be done in submission to and by the authorization of one's senior pastor.

C. Be enthusiastic; keep a celebratory attitude to encourage the people of God about what God is doing through the outreaches and how God is moving through the people of God.

D. Planning outreaches as far out in advance as possible. Make sure, as the Outreach Coordinator, that you have properly authorized the event with your senior pastor with as much notice as possible.

E. Make sure that you have planned with other Outreach Team leaders well in advance.'

F. If you require permission from the housing authorities or other community authorities before carrying-out an outreach, make sure that the proper communication and authorization with those authorities has been carried out well in advance.

G. Rally as much prayer support as possible among the other outreach leaders and church members as far in advance as possible for each outreach.

H. Utilize email blasts, Facebook posts, twitter, and other social media technology to get the word out.

Since you never know what communication channel people will be tuned into, it's important to hit as many of these broadcast methods as possible. This allows you to notify as many people as possible in order to yield the best participation. However, regardless of the initial attendance, God will always honor your faithfulness in the small things and give you the grace to grow from there. This may be the most important key to stewarding consistent outreaches— that is, being faithful, regardless of the turnout.

CULTIVATING A TEAM OF LEADERS

When I was the head student leader of the evangelism student ministry at Christ For The Nations, I quickly learned the importance of an outreach team. An Outreach ministry usually takes many hands in order to make the load light. By discipling a team of outreach leaders around you, you will accomplish multiple goals at one time. Jesus said, "Go therefore and make disciples of all nations, baptizing them in the name of the Father and of the Son and of the Holy Spirit" (Matthew 28:19 ESV).

First, and most importantly, you will be obeying what Jesus commanded you to do by reproducing yourself and equipping the next generation of outreach leaders. Those who you have trained and equipped will never be the same because of your commitment to helping them. Here is a list of strategies on how to better equip those who are around you:

A. Delegate responsibilities to those with leadership potential around you. After they have shown themselves to be faithful in lower levels of responsibility, elevate them gradually into greater and greater levels of responsibility, leadership, and authority. A great goal is to have them one day leading whole outreaches by themselves with the maturity to coordinate and delegate as you have exemplified.

B. Be a source of great encouragement and commendation to those who demonstrate leadership initiative on each occasion.

C. Be perceptive of the skills and passions of those demonstrating leadership initiative. Empower, equip, and release them to take on tasks that fit their individual skill-set and passions. For example, utilize those with administrative skills to handle things like working the database or creating the posters for advertising the outreach. However, those who are bold and fiery, utilize them to teach your first-time outreach participants. Plug each leader in where they are most effective. Also, do this prayerfully, because most importantly, the Holy Spirit will guide you.

D. Always be mindful and remind others that the biblical example of leadership, according to Jesus, is found in Matthew 20:26, "Whoever wants to be a leader among you must be your servant"(NLT). Therefore, those who want to be leaders must become excellent servants on the team and with the local church.

E. Coordinate a consistent meeting time for your team of leaders that is weekly, biweekly, or monthly. There is no formula to this. However, the more frequently you meet with your team, the more united, prayerful, enthusiastic, and organized your outreach ministry will be in general. John Maxwell says, "Everything rises and falls upon leadership."

SUBMIT AND SERVE THE VISION OF THE SENIOR PASTOR

The Bible says in 1 Corinthians 12:13, "For even as the body is one and yet has many members, and all the members of the body, though they are many, are one body, so also is Christ" (ESV). Every member is important to the Body of Christ.

As I previously mentioned in the last chapter, Romans 13:1 says that God has instituted His order and His authority structure in the Church. In order for an evangelist to be appropriately a part of God's authority structure, he or she must be submitted to his or her senior pastor. As it is written, "Everyone must submit himself to the governing authorities" (NIV). The way this looks in the local church setting is that the evangelist, or outreach coordinator, does not operate as a loose cannon or fledgling archer. Everything the Outreach Coordinator does must be done with an awareness of the greater vision that the senior pastor has for the outreach ministry. This is accomplished in several ways.

A. Honor the direction, location, and strategies that the senior pastor has indicated they desire for the

Outreach Ministry on an individual outreach basis or on a general basis.

B. Ask well, thought-out questions and request information from your senior pastor who will help you clarify the expectations and vision that he or she has for the outreaches. Write that information down and obey it. Avoid, at all costs, asking the same question twice or failing to deliver on important outreach details because of a failure to properly record that information.

C. The word for submission in the original Greek New Testament is "hupotassō." This is a military term that literally means to fall into ranks under a leader. When the Scripture says we are to submit to our governing authorities, it literally means that we are to obey the instructions, as if the orders being given were from a higher ranking governing official. In the military, there is no deviation or delay from the officers' original instructions. Failure to do so is considered rebellion or insubordination. In the same way, an Outreach Coordinator should see themselves as an officer in the army of God, who is subject to obeying orders from the higher ranking senior pastor.

OVERSEEING THE FOLLOW-UP

Jesus said, "Follow Me, and I will make you fishers of men." There's no point in catching fish only to throw them back into the river. The Adopt-A-Family Follow Up format was created to empower anyone to be able to bridge the gap between outreach and discipleship. Administrating the follow-up to the new families that are touched through the outreach is essential in making sure that the relationships are long-lasting.

Though an Outreach Coordinator may or may not be a talented administrator, he or she should either learn how to use databasing software, and how to send e-mail broadcasts, or staff someone who does. Regardless of his or her skill level in this area, he or she will need to oversee this process. It may be necessary for him or her to brush up on his/her office skills. Simple word processing with databasing, e-mail broadcasting, basic Facebook event posting, and phone calling should be sufficient administrative skills for this job. Some areas to oversee are:

A. Given that the Community Outreaches are mobilized once a week, an Outreach Coordinator will have to review the First Touch cards from each week to make sure that there is a confirmed Return Visit scheduled. If possible, at least one member of the original group who initially ministered to the family should be a part of the

Return Visit team. This is because having a familiar face on the Return Visit team will make the new family feel more comfortable.

B. The Outreach Coordinator should at least once a week check that the First Touch and Return Visit databases have been updated with new information for each week's follow-up.

C. In the case that someone from the initial First Touch team is not able to make a Return follow-up visit, the Outreach Coordinator should pray about substituting another church member to go for them instead. Ideally, at least one member of the initial Outreach Team should consistently be a part of the weekly Return Visits, so that it matures into a healthy discipleship relationship. The new families will feel most comfortable with seeing a familiar face from the original team.

ENCOURAGING THE BODY TO CELEBRATE OUTREACH AND DISCIPLESHIP

Every Outreach Coordinator should a take a page out of Nehemiah's book. He said, "Go and enjoy choice food and sweet drinks, and send some to those who have nothing prepared. This day is sacred to our Lord. Do not grieve, for the joy of the LORD is your strength" (Nehemiah 8:10 NIV). Nehemiah knew the power of encouraging his team. He sent them to take food to those who were hurting and to go forth with joy. When we commit to acting on God's Word, it is a supreme delight. To see hurting families touched with prayer and God's love, is a true celebration. Even the faith of new families stepping out to be a light to the world is a marvelous occasion. The excitement of reaching the lost with the love of God and the power of God should exude from an Outreach Coordinator. This virtue alone should motivate, inspire, and encourage everyone in the church to want to participate in Community Outreaches.

These are a few of the character traits that serve to make for a great Outreach Coordinator:

A. Have a great attitude, enthusiasm, and anticipation for every Community Outreach.

B. Take a little time when you can to celebrate each person and family from the local church who chooses to participate in the Community Outreaches.

C. At the end of every outreach, gather all the participants together and take time to give each team an opportunity share one or two testimonies from its encounters. As the Outreach Coordinator, emphasize the good, the courageous, the powerful, and the loving steps of faith each team member took. Highlight and celebrate all the good that was done.

D. If, during an outreach, some participants encountered persecution, rejection, or something else that is perceived as a negative, as the leader it is your responsibility to turn it into a positive. Make everything a win-win. For instance, if it was persecution or rejection, point them to the Scripture that states, "Blessed are you that are persecuted for righteousness." Encourage them with the fact that they are in good company with Jesus and all the prophets, and that they can rejoice in doing God's will.

EQUIP THE BODY OF CHRIST TO DO THE SAME

Scripture says in Ephesians 4:11, "He has given some evangelists for the equipping of the saints for the work of ministry unto the building up the body of Christ." Based upon the book of Ephesians, we see the predominant role of an Outreach Coordinator is to train up and equip the saints for the work of ministry. The Outreach Coordinator is not consigned with the exclusive work of soul-winning single-handedly, but is delegated with the work of multiplying soul-winners.

Many congregations have one, two, or maybe a handful of evangelists, but God has not called them only to bring in the Harvest. Many times, it is those who have a strong natural gift in soul-winning that should unite to form an Outreach Leadership Team with the general objective of bringing everyone else up to their level. This can be achieved in several ways:

A. An Outreach Coordinator should have consistent training sessions that church members can attend as a part of a soul winning, Adopt-A-Family Course. This should always be approved under submission to the senior pastor.

B. Possible ideas for training sessions include home groups, mid-week services, weekend workshops, training sessions before an outreach, and Sunday school classes.

C. When conducting training sessions, try not to go longer than 50-60 minutes. People can usually only digest so much in one sitting.

D. Use a well thought out outline for each training session. Use a curriculum like *The American Mission Soulwinner's Manual*. People can find it easier to follow your teaching, if it has strong points.

E. An essential component for equipping is simply consistent outreaches and other outreach experience building exercises.

F. Always encourage church members and other team members to step-out. Always congratulate them for their courage and willingness to take risks to pray for people and share Jesus.

G. The greatest key to remember in training church members is to be the best model and demonstrator of what you are trying to teach. As an Outreach Coordinator, be the first to step out and lead by example.

RELIANCE ON THE HOLY SPIRIT

Though all of these tools will help you be a more effective Outreach Coordinator, one must remember that the greatest quality an Outreach Coordinator can have is his/her reliance on the Holy Spirit. Scripture says, "I am the vine; you are the branches. Whoever abides in me and I in him, he it is that bears much fruit, for apart from me you can do nothing"(John 15:5 ESV).

Unless we seek God to know His will for our community outreach on a daily basis, we will not bear the kind of fruit that remains. Ultimately, the Holy Spirit will help us in every area of our outreach efforts. He is the Master Evangelist. As we get in tune with Him, and strategize our outreaches with His leading, He will give us the awesome results that are mentioned in the Book of Acts when, "The Lord added to their number daily those who were being saved" (Acts 2:47 NIV). Our first priority should be to seek His will and His plan for how He wants us to move forward. Only through His power will we be able to do anything and all of the glory goes to Him.

IN SUMMARY

At the end of the day, being an Outreach Coordinator is serving. Just like it wasn't always fun building my church's website, being an Outreach Coordinator will also have its ups and downs. However, because I was faithful to press through with stewarding the website project, even when I did not want to, God blessed and promoted me. After serving my pastor in that way, it was not long that God began to open up even more doors than ever before in Teen Challenges and churches from around the world for me to be a guest minister.

I honestly believe that if I had not obeyed my pastor in that simple task, the ministry that God has entrusted me with would not be on the same level that it is today.

When we show ourselves trustworthy in a task, even when it does not seem too glamorous to us, God sees it. The Holy Spirit will faithfully reward us for our desire to serve His Body and equip His people. I do not know if the Holy Spirit will reward you exactly the way He has blessed me; however, you can expect to be blessed "exceedingly, abundantly, above all that we ask or think" (Ephesians 3:20 ASV), whether in this life or the life to come.

Chapter 9

ADAPTING THE VISION

The Adopt-A-Family format is based upon the foundation of servanthood. Just as Jesus came as the "servant of all" (Mark 9:35 ESV), so are we called to "become all things to all people, that by all means [we] might save some" (1 Corinthians 9:22 ESV).

In each demographic area the needs, desires, and dynamics of the families are radically different. Paul the Apostle understood this reality and had the wisdom to adapt to each area's specific needs. The *Adopt-A-Family Follow-Up* format is based upon the desire to be a blessing to families, right **where they are**.

In the planning stages of any outreach ministry, it is important to pray and ask God for strategies to best meet the needs of the local community in order to open up the most effective door to the Gospel. The fruitfulness of community outreaches will largely be determined by our sensitivity to the needs of that community. For instance, a middle class area will not necessarily respond to a grocery program with the same receptivity that lower income families who live in an apartment complex would respond.

Just as Jesus said, "Follow me, and I will make you fishers of men"(Mark 4:19 ESV), we must seek the Holy

Spirit's help to know what is the best "fishing bait" to use when we are trying to catch men for Jesus in each demographic area. I wholeheartedly believe that there is the right "fishing bait" to use to reach every kind of individual with the love of Jesus in every community. Those strategies are available, but we must seek the Holy Spirit to give them to us.

The first time I did the equipping meetings in Taiwan, I met an incredible lady; a businesswoman who ran with this concept. I'll never forget the story. She was a member of the congregation of the pastor who had asked me to minister for him. The senior pastor and I sought God about a way to cast a "fishing net" that would effectively draw this particular culture into the church.

The Taiwanese can be very shy and reserved people, but also very honorable and technologically savvy. Depending on the source, reports say that Taiwan is somewhere between 2 to 10% Christian. After seeking God, we believed that for these meetings our great "fishing bait" would be more like a fishing lure. We decided to use iPads. So, we believed the Holy Spirit to provide for four iPads for us to give away, through drawings, during the nightly meetings.

The businesswoman, as I mentioned, took this seriously. She went out and invited a multitude of taxi drivers. As a result, in one meeting, we had 40 taxi drivers in attendance. When the altar call was given to accept Jesus Christ as Lord and Savior, at least 20 of these unsaved, unchurched taxi drivers came forward to become born-again. The value of those 20 souls spending an eternity in Heaven is nowhere near the cost of the roughly $2,500 U.S. dollars that it took to buy those iPads. And to top it all off, quite a few of the drivers were also baptized in the Holy Spirit. Many were physically healed during the prayer ministry from the church. This is the power of seeking the Holy Spirit to find a Divine "fishing bait" when it comes to positively reaching the community. It has supernatural results—and all for His glory!

OUTREACH ADAPTATION

As you may have observed, the Adopt-A-Family Follow-Up format's default service to provide is a grocery service. However, you will notice that on the "First Touch" cards there is a place for "other." In this blank, you can fill-in an alternate service that should be the adapted strategy, decided by the Outreach Coordinator for a particular outreach. Some alternate services that can be provided are as follows:

- Music, Acting, or Dance lessons for middle-class families.
- Sports Camps, Tournaments, or Athletic Lessons for lower-income or middle income families.
- English Lessons for Hispanic, Chinese, Hindu, Buddhist, Muslim or other ethnic families.
- Spanish Tutoring or Classes for middle-class or higher income families.

- Homework Study Groups for lower-income, middle class, or higher income families.
- Home Service for middle class, or higher income families.
  - Fence Painting
  - Grass Mowing
  - Edging Hedges
  - Tree Trimming

Being able to adapt is the key to staying relative, not only to the families that you are trying to reach with the love of Jesus, but it is also necessary for staying relative to your own church community. It's common for members of a church family to not feel very gifted or effective in the area of outreach. Because of this, they will flounder at the idea of participating. It is important to adapt our strategies to incorporate every level of believer to become a meaningful part of each outreach. I have included a list of outreaches that have many roles that believers at any level can participate in.

- Community Letter Drop
  - Believers can drop church flyers, door-to-door, or around a community, inviting people to a church service.
  - Distributing Gospel tracts.
- New Testament or Gospel of John Booklet Give-aways.
- Water Bottle Distribution
  - Church information and invitation can be

on the bottle label
  - Gospel tract can be on the bottle label
- Laundry Love
  - Families bring a stack of quarters they have saved up in a "Family Outreach Jar" to the laundry-mat and purchase people's laundry cycle.
- Block Parties or Apartment Complex Festivals
  - Believers can prepare food and serve families.
  - Believers can sing, dance, play an instrument in a band to reach families.
  - Believers can set up a face-painting booth.
  - Believers can look after a bouncy castle for kids.
  - Believers could man Party Games which can include:
  - Horseshoes
  - Pin-the-tail-on-the-donkey
  - Bottle-Cap Ring Toss
  - Hole-in-One
  - Get Creative!

The common, inner struggle and resistance in the heart of believers to stepping out into an outreach can be diffused within one or two positive experiences. Many believers have made a decision to not do outreaches, without even giving it a single attempt. By encouraging believers to participate in an outreach event in a capacity that does not seem confrontational to them, one will enable them to see how easy it is to get started in such a rewarding experience without reinforcing their resistance to talk to strangers.

God will do a wonderful work in them as they take a step of faith and see the corresponding impact their initiative makes on families in the community. Those families touched by their participation will never be the same. Undoubtedly, those who were initially hesitant will also become softened in their hearts and reinforced with courage to keep stepping out because of their positive experience of being a part of a winning outreach team.

HOW TO ADAPT THE ADOPT-A-FAMILY APPROACH

Regardless of the outreach strategy, the basic format from the Adopt-A-Family format should be uniform or consistent. This Follow-Up format consists of five parts.

- The initial conversation and witnessing encounter.
- The invitation to participate in a service that meets a "felt" need of the individual or family.
  - Services May Include: Groceries, Lessons, Lawn Service, Tutoring, etc.
- The documentation of the family or individual's contact information on the "First Touch" card.
- The documentation and scheduling of the follow-up service to be provided on the "First Touch" card.

- The return visit to continue the pattern of providing that service on a weekly basis, thus opening the door for a long-term relationship.

In order to practice what Jesus instructed us to do in His Word, "That your fruit would remain" (Mark 15:16 NASB), we must show due diligence, and properly record the follow-up information of those families who we encounter. Our first encounter is only the beginning of a wonderful relationship to help people grow in their closeness to Jesus. The "First Touch" card empowers us to document their contact information, in an organized way, which will facilitate our future communication with them on an individual level and at a local church level.

So, regardless of what adaptation is applied, be sure to follow the same pattern of setting an appointment to deliver the service at a future time. The best return visit location will always be at their home because they are least likely to be a "no-show" at that location.

The service that you obliged to offer is simply a window of opportunity to serve them, as Jesus taught us to do, and to continue to get to know the family and pray with them. In order for the best results, the Return Visit should be ministered as regularly as possible.

As outreaches are extended to minister to families in the communities, be sure to utilize the full benefit of the Adopt-A-Family Follow-Up format by cataloging all follow-up information. Be sure to properly steward the Harvest God gives you by recording family information into the Adopt-A-Family Handbook for each encounter and submitting First Touch Cards and Return Visit Cards to the Outreach Coordinator to update your Community Outreach Databases.

I WILL NEVER FORGET

I will never forget my first visit to Taiwan. It was such a miraculous experience with the power of God moving every night, healing physical illnesses, delivering people from bondages, and souls getting right with Jesus. Of all the stories that marked my life from that trip, there is one that stands out in my mind. It is of a woman that we passed by in the M.R.T. railway station. She was walking along with a little girl, but she seemed lost and confused, like she was looking for something. For some reason, she kind of stared at me as we were walking by. Maybe it might have been because I was the only Anglo around, but on second thought, I think it was the Holy Spirit. Furthermore, for some reason, her face seemed illuminated to me.

In a hurry, walking behind Momma Lydia's athletic stride to the church service, I soon forgot about her, as we pressed through the crowds to reach our train. When we arrived at the church, we prayed and prepared for the service. I was eventually called up to bring the message for the night. Out of the corner of my eye, I noticed a familiar face. When I gave the altar call for those to come forward to receive Jesus as Lord and Savior that night, my jaw dropped. Here was the same woman and little girl I saw at the train station. She was standing at the altar, waiting to receive Jesus. She had followed me to the service!

My heart rejoiced at the goodness of God. Even though I had not initiated any direct interaction with this woman, the Holy Spirit Himself had drawn her to follow me right into the church. Without my even me knowing it, He had led her right to the altar to receive Jesus. Scripture says, "No one can come to me unless the Father who sent me draws him. I will raise him up on the last day" (John 6:44 ESV). I was just a bystander, and the Holy Spirit did what only He could do, regardless of me.

This is what we must always remember; it's the Holy Spirit Who is the only One Who can do the work of salvation. We are just players on the field, but He's the One Who scores all the goals. Without Him, we truly can do nothing, as His word says, "For apart from me you can do nothing" (John 15:5 ESV).

Although this format is an approach that gives families the language, starting point, and strategies to connect with families for the purpose of sharing the love of Jesus with them, ultimately, it is the Holy Spirit Who is the only One Who can move with such an approach to make it successful. We are just the bystanders, and our plans are only in part, but the Holy Spirit will show us the perfect, as we seek Him and open ourselves up to His guidance. This is why I strongly encourage, as the author, spirit-filled, prayerful adaptation of this Adopt-A-Family format wherever the Holy Spirit chooses to use it.

BE LIKE JESUS

One time, a critic had his heart set on tearing down the concept of feeding and ministering to people's needs as an effort to reach them with the Gospel. His insight was … "Shouldn't the Gospel be enough?" However, in his critique, he made a comment that reversed his case. His words were, "When people came to see Jesus, they came for dinner and a show." If even Jesus creatively ministered to the people's needs to eat physical food so that He could share the gospel with them, how much more should we, because He is our example. The Bible says, "Jesus then took the loaves, gave thanks, and distributed to those who were seated as much as they wanted. He did the same with the fish" (John 6:11 ESV).

In your journey to answer the call from Jesus to disciple and be a family that reaches hurting families through serving them and faithfully being their Christian friend, don't let anyone or anything ever take away your confidence.

Hebrews 10:35, "So do not throw away your confidence; it will be richly rewarded" (NIV).

ABOUT THE AUTHOR

Rev. Anthony Dee went from being a Catholic to an Atheist to a Pentecostal Christian. Ten years ago, he was born-again in a movie theatre while watching the movie, *Passion Of The Christ*, and became Spirit filled. Immediately he answered the call to preach the Gospel. An earmark of his ministry is the signs and wonders that follow him, validated with medical records.

A Christ For The Nations graduate, he has now taught in Bible Schools and churches around the world. Since that time, God has sent him to do missions' work in Israel, South Africa, Zimbabwe, and Taiwan. He has also ministered at 15 Teen Challenge Centers in 8 states; The Wisdom Center with Dr. Mike Murdoch; Christ For The Nations Institute—as a guest speaker (6 times) and The Voice of Healing Conference and classes, which included the healings and miracles class. He has been a Guest Speaker at the International House of Prayer in Kansas City, Missouri; Faith World Bible School, Bishop Monjoro, Harare Zimbabwe.

Rev. Anthony Dee is currently on the pastoral staff at River of Life Church, (Staff Five-Fold Evangelist). He has personally been the Guest Speaker in over 30 churches inside the United States, including the Assemblies of God, Full-Gospel Fellowship, International Convention of Faith Ministries, Baptist, Praise Chapel, and non-denominational Churches.

Rev. Anthony Dee has an A.A. degree in Bible (Southwestern Assemblies of God University), a B.S. degree in Professional Development (SAGU), a 3rd-Year Diploma from the Advanced School of Leadership and Pastoral (Christ for the Nations Institute), a 2-Year Diploma in Practical Theology (CFNI). He graduated from the Reinhard Bonnke School of Evangelism.

Besides teaching in Bible Schools and internationally known churches around the world, God has used him to equip the Body of Christ in the area of outreach through his book, *The American Mission: Soulwinner's Manual.* His greatest credential, however, is the Holy Spirit anointing that he walks in and his unwavering desire to give Jesus all of the glory.

CONTACT INFORMATION

Web: www.anthonydee.com

E-mail: anthonydeeministries@gmail.com

Phone: 214-886-0987

Address:
7803 Zoar Ave.
Lubbock, TX 79424

INDEX

FIRST TOUCH CARD

🏠🏠🏠
ADOPT-A-FAMILY

FIRST Touch Card   WWW.ANTHONYDEE.COM

Complex Name: _____ **Date:** ___/___/____

(**Circle** Choices)

1. **Groceries?** Yes / No **Other**: _____	1. **Groceries?** Yes / No **Other**: _____
2. **Return** Time: ___:___ PM / AM	2. **Return** Time: ___:___ PM / AM
Day of Week: **M T W Th F S Su**	Day of Week: **M T W Th F S Su**
3. Attend **Church**: Yes / No	3. Attend **Church**: Yes / No
4. Morning **Pick Up**: Yes / No	4. Morning **Pick Up**: Yes / No

Contact Info:

1. **Name: F**_____ **L**_____

2. **Address**:_____
_____

Bldg. #: _____   **Apt #:** _____

3. **Cell:** _____ - _____ - _____

4. **E-Mail**: _____

5. **Facebook:** Yes / No

6. F.B. E-Mail **Name:** _____

Contact Info:

1. **Name: F**_____ **L**_____

2. **Address**:_____
_____

Bldg. #: _____   **Apt #:** _____

3. **Cell:** _____ - _____ - _____

4. **E-Mail**: _____

5. **Facebook:** Yes / No

6. F.B. Email **Name:** _____

Original **Team** Members:_____

RETURN VISIT CARD

RETURN Visit Card   WWW.ANTHONYDEE.COM

ADOPT-A-FAMILY

Complex Name: _____ **Date:** __/__/____

(**Circle** Choices)

Contact Info:

Info Change Since Last Visit? **Yes / No**

1. **Name**: F_____ L_____
2. **Spouse:** _____
3. **Address:**_____
   _____

Bldg. #: _____   **Apt #:** _____

4. **Cell:** _____ - _____ - _____
5. **E-Mail**: _____
6. Names of **Kids:**_____
   _____

7. Areas of **Struggle:** _____
   _____
   _____

For **Next Visit**:

1. **Groceries?** Yes / No **Other**: _____
2. **Return** Time: ____:____ PM / AM
   Day of Week: **M T W Th F S Su**
3. Attend **Church**: Yes / No
4. Morning **Pick Up**: Yes / No

Other **Information**

1. **Number** of Return **Visits:** _____
2. Date of **Last Return** Visit:_____
3. **Prayer** Requests:_____
   _____
   _____
4. **Answered** Prayer **Requests:**
   _____
   _____

Family Members On **This Visit**:_____

ADDRESS BOOK

PRAYER BOARD